I NEED TO UNPLUG

Created and published by Knock Knock
Distributed by Who's There Inc.
Venice, CA 90291
knockknockstuff.com

© 2014 Who's There Inc.
All rights reserved
Knock Knock is a trademark of Who's There Inc.
Made in China

ISBN: 978-160106581-0
UPC: 825703-50030-1

10 9 8 7 6 5 4 3 2

DO YOU
SEE SCREENS WHEN

you close your eyes? Freak out when there's no cellphone reception? Keep hitting refresh on Facebook like a rat in a Skinner box? Are you beginning to think that this may be a problem?

Enough with the digital distractions—the Internet, the smartphone, the dumb phone, the video games, the TV, the tablet! All that noise, all that information, all those questions. It's all too much. You need quiet. You need to think. You need to unplug. Is there anywhere in this world of 24/7 connectivity where you can get a moment of peace?

There's a consensus growing among the mental health community that all of this connectivity is making us nuts. According to the *New York Times*, the barrage of information that bombards us via technology can affect the way we think and damage our ability to focus. We're hardwired to respond to new things coming at us—information, opportunities, threats—and the thrill is addictive; it actually gives us a minor dopamine hit. When the novelty stops, we don't know what to do with ourselves. Multitasking makes it harder to decide what information is worth noting and what's worth ignoring. We can't concentrate, our thoughts get fractured, and we get stressed out. *Forbes Magazine* also asserts that it's only a matter of time before Internet addiction is classified as a disorder.

The Internet didn't bring about the concept of unplugging. People have felt the urge to disconnect for generations, even before technology took over our lives. In the seventeenth century, philosopher Blaise Pascal wrote, "All of man's problems come from his inability to sit quietly in a room alone." Pascal probably wouldn't be a big fan of social media. Henry David Thoreau took to the woods around Walden Pond in the 1840s seeking a Spartan simplicity away from the distractions of civilization. We can assume he would have left his smartphone behind if he'd had one: "Our inventions are wont to be pretty toys, which distract our attention from serious things."

The telephone wasn't around very long before people started hating on it. In the *Devil's Dictionary*, Ambrose Bierce called it "an invention of the devil," and Mark Twain is famous for his Christmas message wishing "everlasting rest and peace and bliss" to everyone "except the inventor of the telephone."

In the last century or so, the antitechnology chatter has been constant. Ironically, the Internet is full of articles on why the technology barrage is bad for you and how to disconnect. But you don't need to know why you should unplug. You've got this journal, and it's time to make the break.

A journal—besides being a tool for quiet, technology-free contemplation—has been shown to have other powerful benefits. As self-help guru Deepak Chopra claims, "Journaling is one of the most powerful tools we have to transform our lives," and there is consistent evidence that journal-writing aids physical health. According to a widely cited study by James W. Pennebaker and Janel D. Seagal, "Writing about important personal experiences in an emotional way...brings about improvements in mental and physical health." Proven benefits include better stress management, strengthened immune systems, fewer doctor visits, and improvement in chronic illnesses such as asthma.

It's not entirely clear how journaling accomplishes all this. Catharsis is involved, but many also point to the value of organizing experiences into a cohesive narrative. According to *Newsweek*, some experts believe that journaling "forces us to transform the ruminations cluttering our minds into coherent stories."

As a devotee of this journal, you most likely know its value. But what's the best way to use it? Specialists agree that in order to reap the benefits of journaling you have to stick with it, quasi-daily, for as little as five minutes at a time (at least fifteen minutes, however, is best). Turning off the gadgets and getting starting is the hardest part.

If you find yourself unable come up with something to write, and the Web is calling your name, don't stress. Think of it as a blog or Pinterest, except it's not online and is meant for your eyes only. Try stream of consciousness—let the thoughts float through you. Describe what's in front of you. Write about what you love. Write a conversation that you might have with someone you admire (or someone you can't stand). Write about the technology-free adventures you'd like to take. Draw. Use the quotes in the journal as a jumping-off point for observations and explorations. Write whatever comes, and don't criticize it; journaling is a means of self-reflection, not a structured composition. In other words, spew.

Beware: a red line will not appear under words you misspell. When you turn the page, you won't find a browser to look something up. You may not be the first to tweet when someone famous dies or the first to like your friend's clever post. But writing offline has lots of perks. Internet trolls won't make nasty comments and your mom won't stumble across it. Your kid won't sit next to you demanding to see that funny dog video for the 234th time. You won't have to turn off your journal when the plane is taking off and landing.

Determine a good home for your journal, such as on top of the TV or near your phone charger, where you can reference it with ease when you're feeling overwhelmed by the ever-encroaching screen. You don't have to go nuts and unplug completely. (People who do that are a little crazy, not to mention really hard to reach.) But a digital break every now and again will do you serious good. And, believe it or not, your gizmos won't even miss you.

You think that machine is your friend, but it's not.

NORA EPHRON

DATE		

WHY I NEED TO UNPLUG TODAY:

_____

_____

_____

_____

_____

_____

_____

_____

_____

_____

_____

_____

_____

_____

_____

_____

_____

_____

_____

_____

_____

_____

DIGITAL DISTRACTIONS TO AVOID TODAY:

Everybody gets so much information all day long that they lose their common sense.

GERTRUDE STEIN

DATE		

WHY I NEED TO UNPLUG TODAY:

_____

_____

_____

_____

_____

_____

_____

_____

_____

_____

_____

_____

_____

_____

_____

_____

_____

_____

_____

_____

_____

_____

DIGITAL DISTRACTIONS TO AVOID TODAY:

Your mind will answer most questions if you learn to relax and wait for the answer.

WILLIAM S. BURROUGHS

DATE		

WHY I NEED TO UNPLUG TODAY:

_____

_____

_____

_____

_____

_____

_____

_____

_____

_____

_____

_____

_____

_____

_____

_____

_____

_____

_____

_____

_____

DIGITAL DISTRACTIONS TO AVOID TODAY:

The Internet also makes it extraordinarily difficult for me to focus. One small break to look up exactly how almond milk is made, and four hours later I'm reading about the Donner Party and texting all my friends: DID YOU GUYS KNOW ABOUT THE DONNER PARTY AND HOW MESSED UP THAT WAS?

MINDY KALING

DATE		

WHY I NEED TO UNPLUG TODAY:

_____

_____

_____

_____

_____

_____

_____

_____

_____

_____

_____

_____

_____

_____

_____

_____

_____

_____

_____

_____

_____

_____

_____

DIGITAL DISTRACTIONS TO AVOID TODAY:

Life moves pretty fast. If you don't stop and look around once in a while, you could miss it.

JOHN HUGHES

WHY I NEED TO UNPLUG TODAY:

_____

_____

_____

_____

_____

_____

_____

_____

_____

_____

_____

_____

_____

_____

_____

_____

_____

_____

_____

_____

_____

_____

_____

DIGITAL DISTRACTIONS TO AVOID TODAY:

There must be quite a few things that a hot bath won't cure, but I don't know many of them.

SYLVIA PLATH

DATE

WHY I NEED TO UNPLUG TODAY:

_____

_____

_____

_____

_____

_____

_____

_____

_____

_____

_____

_____

_____

_____

_____

_____

_____

_____

_____

_____

_____

_____

DIGITAL DISTRACTIONS TO AVOID TODAY:

[Computers] are useless. They can only give you answers.

PABLO PICASSO

DATE

WHY I NEED TO UNPLUG TODAY:

_____

_____

_____

_____

_____

_____

_____

_____

_____

_____

_____

_____

_____

_____

_____

_____

_____

_____

_____

_____

DIGITAL DISTRACTIONS TO AVOID TODAY:

There's never enough time to do all the nothing you want.

BILL WATTERSON

DATE		

WHY I NEED TO UNPLUG TODAY:

_____

_____

_____

_____

_____

_____

_____

_____

_____

_____

_____

_____

_____

_____

_____

_____

_____

_____

_____

_____

_____

_____

_____

_____

DIGITAL DISTRACTIONS TO AVOID TODAY:

We are now part of this giant machine where every second we have to take out a device and contribute our thoughts and opinions.

GARY SHTEYNGART

WHY I NEED TO UNPLUG TODAY:

_____

_____

_____

_____

_____

_____

_____

_____

_____

_____

_____

_____

_____

_____

_____

_____

_____

_____

_____

_____

_____

_____

_____

_____

DIGITAL DISTRACTIONS TO AVOID TODAY:

Production of too many useful things produces too large a *useless* population.

KARL MARX

DATE

WHY I NEED TO UNPLUG TODAY:

_____

_____

_____

_____

_____

_____

_____

_____

_____

_____

_____

_____

_____

_____

_____

_____

_____

_____

_____

_____

_____

_____

DIGITAL DISTRACTIONS TO AVOID TODAY:

I would trade all
of my technology
for an afternoon
with Socrates.

STEVE JOBS

WHY I NEED TO UNPLUG TODAY:

_____

_____

_____

_____

_____

_____

_____

_____

_____

_____

_____

_____

_____

_____

_____

_____

_____

_____

_____

_____

_____

_____

_____

_____

_____

DIGITAL DISTRACTIONS TO AVOID TODAY:

We didn't have Facebook when I was growing up. We had "phonebook," but you wouldn't waste an afternoon on it.

———

BETTY WHITE

WHY I NEED TO UNPLUG TODAY:

_____

_____

_____

_____

_____

_____

_____

_____

_____

_____

_____

_____

_____

_____

_____

_____

_____

_____

_____

_____

_____

_____

DIGITAL DISTRACTIONS TO AVOID TODAY:

What good is knowledge if it just floats in the air? It goes from computer to computer. It changes and grows every second of every day. But nobody actually knows anything.

DON DELILLO

WHY I NEED TO UNPLUG TODAY:

_____

_____

_____

_____

_____

_____

_____

_____

_____

_____

_____

_____

_____

_____

_____

_____

_____

_____

_____

_____

_____

_____

DIGITAL DISTRACTIONS TO AVOID TODAY:

"God, don't they teach you how to spell these days?"
"No," I answer. "They teach us to use spell-check."

JODI PICOULT

DATE		

WHY I NEED TO UNPLUG TODAY:

_____

_____

_____

_____

_____

_____

_____

_____

_____

_____

_____

_____

_____

_____

_____

_____

_____

_____

_____

_____

_____

_____

_____

DIGITAL DISTRACTIONS TO AVOID TODAY:

I've always been afraid of video games—not afraid that I wouldn't like them, but that I would like them too much, and that after mere seconds in front of any particularly bright and absorbing game, I would abandon all ambition, turn into a mouth-breathing zombie, and develop a wide, sofa-shaped rear end.

SUSAN ORLEAN

DATE		

WHY I NEED TO UNPLUG TODAY:

_____

_____

_____

_____

_____

_____

_____

_____

_____

_____

_____

_____

_____

_____

_____

_____

_____

_____

_____

_____

_____

DIGITAL DISTRACTIONS TO AVOID TODAY:

There are many things of which a wise man would wish to be ignorant.

RALPH WALDO EMERSON

DATE		

WHY I NEED TO UNPLUG TODAY:

_____

_____

_____

_____

_____

_____

_____

_____

_____

_____

_____

_____

_____

_____

_____

_____

_____

_____

_____

_____

_____

_____

_____

DIGITAL DISTRACTIONS TO AVOID TODAY:

Do you sometimes look up from the computer and look around the room and know you are alone, I mean really know it, then feel scared?

TAO LIN

WHY I NEED TO UNPLUG TODAY:

_____

_____

_____

_____

_____

_____

_____

_____

_____

_____

_____

_____

_____

_____

_____

_____

_____

_____

_____

_____

_____

_____

_____

_____

DIGITAL DISTRACTIONS TO AVOID TODAY:

It rots the senses in the head!
It kills imagination dead!
His brain becomes as soft as cheese!
His powers of thinking rust and freeze!

ROALD DAHL

WHY I NEED TO UNPLUG TODAY:

_____

_____

_____

_____

_____

_____

_____

_____

_____

_____

_____

_____

_____

_____

_____

_____

_____

_____

_____

_____

_____

_____

_____

DIGITAL DISTRACTIONS TO AVOID TODAY:

To sit in the shade on a fine day, and look upon verdure, is the most perfect refreshment.

JANE AUSTEN

DATE		

WHY I NEED TO UNPLUG TODAY:

_____

_____

_____

_____

_____

_____

_____

_____

_____

_____

_____

_____

_____

_____

_____

_____

_____

_____

_____

_____

_____

_____

DIGITAL DISTRACTIONS TO AVOID TODAY:

I am in love with
the world ... It is a
blessing to find the
time to do the things,
to read the books, to
listen to the music.

MAURICE SENDAK

DATE		

WHY I NEED TO UNPLUG TODAY:

_____

_____

_____

_____

_____

_____

_____

_____

_____

_____

_____

_____

_____

_____

_____

_____

_____

_____

_____

_____

_____

_____

_____

_____

DIGITAL DISTRACTIONS TO AVOID TODAY:

My first impulse, when presented with any spanking-new piece of computer hardware, is to imagine how it will look in ten years' time, gathering dust under a card table in a thrift shop.

———————

WILLIAM GIBSON

DATE

WHY I NEED TO UNPLUG TODAY:

_____

_____

_____

_____

_____

_____

_____

_____

_____

_____

_____

_____

_____

_____

_____

_____

_____

_____

_____

_____

_____

_____

_____

_____

DIGITAL DISTRACTIONS TO AVOID TODAY:

I do think that
socializing on
the Internet is
to socializing
what reality
TV is to reality.

AARON SORKIN

DATE		

WHY I NEED TO UNPLUG TODAY:

_____

_____

_____

_____

_____

_____

_____

_____

_____

_____

_____

_____

_____

_____

_____

_____

_____

_____

_____

_____

_____

DIGITAL DISTRACTIONS TO AVOID TODAY:

It's a very difficult era in which to be a person, just a real, actual person, instead of a collection of personality traits selected from an endless Automat of characters.

———————

GILLIAN FLYNN

DATE		

WHY I NEED TO UNPLUG TODAY:

_____

_____

_____

_____

_____

_____

_____

_____

_____

_____

_____

_____

_____

_____

_____

_____

_____

_____

_____

_____

_____

DIGITAL DISTRACTIONS TO AVOID TODAY:

If we amplify everything, we hear nothing.

JON STEWART

DATE		

WHY I NEED TO UNPLUG TODAY:

_____

_____

_____

_____

_____

_____

_____

_____

_____

_____

_____

_____

_____

_____

_____

_____

_____

_____

_____

_____

_____

_____

_____

_____

DIGITAL DISTRACTIONS TO AVOID TODAY:

Instructions for living a life:
Pay attention.
Be astonished.
Tell about it.

MARY OLIVER

DATE	

WHY I NEED TO UNPLUG TODAY:

_____

_____

_____

_____

_____

_____

_____

_____

_____

_____

_____

_____

_____

_____

_____

_____

_____

_____

_____

_____

_____

_____

DIGITAL DISTRACTIONS TO AVOID TODAY:

In the age of Google, when everything you say is forever searchable, the future belongs to those who leave no footprints.

THOMAS L. FRIEDMAN

DATE		

WHY I NEED TO UNPLUG TODAY:

_____
_____
_____
_____
_____
_____
_____
_____
_____
_____
_____
_____
_____
_____
_____
_____
_____
_____
_____
_____
_____
_____
_____

DIGITAL DISTRACTIONS TO AVOID TODAY:

The twentieth century has built up a powerful set of intellectual shortcuts and devices that help us defend ourselves against moments when clouds suddenly appear to think.

CHARLES BAXTER

	DATE	

WHY I NEED TO UNPLUG TODAY:

_____

_____

_____

_____

_____

_____

_____

_____

_____

_____

_____

_____

_____

_____

_____

_____

_____

_____

_____

_____

_____

_____

_____

_____

_____

DIGITAL DISTRACTIONS TO AVOID TODAY:

Why do we pursue information that we know will never leave our heads?

DAVE EGGERS

DATE

WHY I NEED TO UNPLUG TODAY:

_____

_____

_____

_____

_____

_____

_____

_____

_____

_____

_____

_____

_____

_____

_____

_____

_____

_____

_____

_____

_____

_____

_____

_____

_____

DIGITAL DISTRACTIONS TO AVOID TODAY:

Men have become the tools of their tools.

HENRY DAVID THOREAU

DATE		

WHY I NEED TO UNPLUG TODAY:

_____

_____

_____

_____

_____

_____

_____

_____

_____

_____

_____

_____

_____

_____

_____

_____

_____

_____

_____

_____

_____

DIGITAL DISTRACTIONS TO AVOID TODAY:

In wildness I sense the miracle of life, and beside it our scientific accomplishments fade to trivia.

CHARLES A. LINDBERGH

DATE		

WHY I NEED TO UNPLUG TODAY:

_____

_____

_____

_____

_____

_____

_____

_____

_____

_____

_____

_____

_____

_____

_____

_____

_____

_____

_____

_____

_____

_____

_____

_____

DIGITAL DISTRACTIONS TO AVOID TODAY:

I have to tell you I *love* living in a world without clocks. The shackles are gone. I'm a puppy unleashed in a meadow of time.

JERRY SPINELLI

DATE		

WHY I NEED TO UNPLUG TODAY:

_____

_____

_____

_____

_____

_____

_____

_____

_____

_____

_____

_____

_____

_____

_____

_____

_____

_____

_____

_____

_____

_____

DIGITAL DISTRACTIONS TO AVOID TODAY:

Anyone who's grown up listening to albums and then to CDs can't help but feel sad about the atomization of music consumption. It would be like if we couldn't publish a book anymore, only chapters.

JENNIFER EGAN

DATE

WHY I NEED TO UNPLUG TODAY:

_____

_____

_____

_____

_____

_____

_____

_____

_____

_____

_____

_____

_____

_____

_____

_____

_____

_____

_____

_____

_____

_____

_____

_____

_____

_____

DIGITAL DISTRACTIONS TO AVOID TODAY:

It's doubtful that anyone with an Internet connection at his workplace is writing good fiction.

JONATHAN FRANZEN

DATE		

HOW I'M WORKING ON MYSELF TODAY:

_____

_____

_____

_____

_____

_____

_____

_____

_____

_____

_____

_____

_____

_____

_____

_____

_____

_____

_____

_____

_____

_____

_____

TODAY'S PERSONAL OUTLOOK:

This was before voice mail, recorded phone messages you can't escape. Life was easier then. You just didn't pick up the phone.

JOYCE CAROL OATES

DATE		

WHY I NEED TO UNPLUG TODAY:

_____
_____
_____
_____
_____
_____
_____
_____
_____
_____
_____
_____
_____
_____
_____
_____
_____
_____
_____
_____
_____
_____
_____
_____
_____

DIGITAL DISTRACTIONS TO AVOID TODAY:

Call me naive, but I seem to have underestimated the universal desire to sit in a hard plastic chair and stare at a screen until your eyes cross.

DAVID SEDARIS

DATE		

HOW I'M WORKING ON MYSELF TODAY:

_____

_____

_____

_____

_____

_____

_____

_____

_____

_____

_____

_____

_____

_____

_____

_____

_____

_____

_____

_____

_____

_____

_____

_____

_____

TODAY'S PERSONAL OUTLOOK:

I have lived on the lip of insanity,
wanting to know reasons, knocking
on a door. It opens. I've been knocking
from the inside!

___

RUMI

DATE		

WHY I NEED TO UNPLUG TODAY:

_____

_____

_____

_____

_____

_____

_____

_____

_____

_____

_____

_____

_____

_____

_____

_____

_____

_____

_____

_____

_____

_____

_____

DIGITAL DISTRACTIONS TO AVOID TODAY:

Man's curiosity, his relentlessness, his inventiveness, his ingenuity have led him into deep trouble. We can only hope that these same traits will enable him to claw his way out.

E. B. WHITE

WHY I NEED TO UNPLUG TODAY:

_____

_____

_____

_____

_____

_____

_____

_____

_____

_____

_____

_____

_____

_____

_____

_____

_____

_____

_____

_____

_____

DIGITAL DISTRACTIONS TO AVOID TODAY:

People miss so much because they want money and comfort and pride, a house and a job to pay for the house. And they have to get a car. You can't see anything from a car. It's moving too fast. People take vacations. That's their reward—the vacation. Why not the life?

JACK GILBERT

DATE		

WHY I NEED TO UNPLUG TODAY:

_____

_____

_____

_____

_____

_____

_____

_____

_____

_____

_____

_____

_____

_____

_____

_____

_____

_____

_____

_____

_____

_____

DIGITAL DISTRACTIONS TO AVOID TODAY:

I sometimes wonder whether all pleasures are not substitutes for joy.

C. S. LEWIS

DATE		

WHY I NEED TO UNPLUG TODAY:

_____

_____

_____

_____

_____

_____

_____

_____

_____

_____

_____

_____

_____

_____

_____

_____

_____

_____

_____

_____

_____

_____

DIGITAL DISTRACTIONS TO AVOID TODAY:

Then, I turned around and walked to my room and closed my door and put my head under my pillow and let the quiet put things where they are supposed to be.

STEPHEN CHBOSKY

	DATE	

WHY I NEED TO UNPLUG TODAY:

_____

_____

_____

_____

_____

_____

_____

_____

_____

_____

_____

_____

_____

_____

_____

_____

_____

_____

_____

_____

_____

DIGITAL DISTRACTIONS TO AVOID TODAY:

I know there's a proverb which says "To err is human," but a human error is nothing to what a computer can do if it tries.

AGATHA CHRISTIE

DATE		

WHY I NEED TO UNPLUG TODAY:

_____

_____

_____

_____

_____

_____

_____

_____

_____

_____

_____

_____

_____

_____

_____

_____

_____

_____

_____

_____

_____

_____

DIGITAL DISTRACTIONS TO AVOID TODAY:

Besides the noble art of getting things done, there is a nobler art of leaving things undone.

LIN YUTANG

DATE

WHY I NEED TO UNPLUG TODAY:

_____

_____

_____

_____

_____

_____

_____

_____

_____

_____

_____

_____

_____

_____

_____

_____

_____

_____

_____

_____

_____

_____

_____

_____

_____

DIGITAL DISTRACTIONS TO AVOID TODAY:

Even the technology that promises to unite us, divides us. Each of us is now electronically connected to the globe, and yet we feel utterly alone.

DAN BROWN

	DATE	

WHY I NEED TO UNPLUG TODAY:

_____

_____

_____

_____

_____

_____

_____

_____

_____

_____

_____

_____

_____

_____

_____

_____

_____

_____

_____

_____

_____

_____

_____

DIGITAL DISTRACTIONS TO AVOID TODAY:

Perhaps the truth depends on a walk around the lake.

WALLACE STEVENS

DATE		

WHY I NEED TO UNPLUG TODAY:

_____

_____

_____

_____

_____

_____

_____

_____

_____

_____

_____

_____

_____

_____

_____

_____

_____

_____

_____

_____

_____

_____

_____

_____

DIGITAL DISTRACTIONS TO AVOID TODAY:

I started to distrust telephones the instant they stopped working. I can't pinpoint when that was—the first time I "dropped" a call, or someone said, "I'm losing you."

VIRGINIA HEFFERNAN

DATE		

WHY I NEED TO UNPLUG TODAY:

_____

_____

_____

_____

_____

_____

_____

_____

_____

_____

_____

_____

_____

_____

_____

_____

_____

_____

_____

_____

DIGITAL DISTRACTIONS TO AVOID TODAY:

And it occurred to me that in this new millennial life of instant and ubiquitous connection, you don't in fact communicate so much as leave messages for one another.

———

CHANG-RAE LEE

	DATE	

WHY I NEED TO UNPLUG TODAY:

_____

_____

_____

_____

_____

_____

_____

_____

_____

_____

_____

_____

_____

_____

_____

_____

_____

_____

_____

_____

_____

DIGITAL DISTRACTIONS TO AVOID TODAY:

I began to see my body like an iPad or a car. I would drive it and demand things from it. It had no limits. It was invincible.

EVE ENSLER

DATE		

WHY I NEED TO UNPLUG TODAY:

_____

_____

_____

_____

_____

_____

_____

_____

_____

_____

_____

_____

_____

_____

_____

_____

_____

_____

_____

_____

_____

_____

DIGITAL DISTRACTIONS TO AVOID TODAY:

Creativity— like human life itself— begins in darkness.

JULIA CAMERON

DATE

WHY I NEED TO UNPLUG TODAY:

_____
_____
_____
_____
_____
_____
_____
_____
_____
_____
_____
_____
_____
_____
_____
_____
_____
_____
_____
_____
_____
_____
_____

DIGITAL DISTRACTIONS TO AVOID TODAY:

[E-mail] has some magical ability to turn off the politeness gene in the human being.

JEFF BEZOS

DATE		

WHY I NEED TO UNPLUG TODAY:

_____

_____

_____

_____

_____

_____

_____

_____

_____

_____

_____

_____

_____

_____

_____

_____

_____

_____

_____

_____

_____

_____

_____

_____

DIGITAL DISTRACTIONS TO AVOID TODAY:

Life changes
in the instant.

JOAN DIDION

WHY I NEED TO UNPLUG TODAY:

_____

_____

_____

_____

_____

_____

_____

_____

_____

_____

_____

_____

_____

_____

_____

_____

_____

_____

_____

_____

_____

_____

_____

_____

DIGITAL DISTRACTIONS TO AVOID TODAY:

I only went out for a walk, and finally concluded to stay out till sundown, for going out, I found, was really going in.

JOHN MUIR

DATE		

WHY I NEED TO UNPLUG TODAY:

_____

_____

_____

_____

_____

_____

_____

_____

_____

_____

_____

_____

_____

_____

_____

_____

_____

_____

_____

_____

_____

DIGITAL DISTRACTIONS TO AVOID TODAY:

When I leave my car my iPhone escorts me, letting everyone else in the post office know that I'm not really with them, I'm with my own people, who are so hilarious that I can't help smiling to myself as I text them back.

MIRANDA JULY

DATE		

WHY I NEED TO UNPLUG TODAY:

_____

_____

_____

_____

_____

_____

_____

_____

_____

_____

_____

_____

_____

_____

_____

_____

_____

_____

_____

_____

_____

_____

_____

DIGITAL DISTRACTIONS TO AVOID TODAY:

Turn off your mind, relax, and float downstream.

JOHN LENNON

DATE		

WHY I NEED TO UNPLUG TODAY:

_____

_____

_____

_____

_____

_____

_____

_____

_____

_____

_____

_____

_____

_____

_____

_____

_____

_____

_____

_____

_____

_____

_____

_____

_____

_____

_____

DIGITAL DISTRACTIONS TO AVOID TODAY:

Life without a phone is riskier, lonelier, more vivid.

————————

ELOISA JAMES

DATE		

WHY I NEED TO UNPLUG TODAY:

_____
_____
_____
_____
_____
_____
_____
_____
_____
_____
_____
_____
_____
_____
_____
_____
_____
_____
_____
_____
_____
_____
_____

DIGITAL DISTRACTIONS TO AVOID TODAY:

And forget not that the earth delights to feel your bare feet and the winds long to play with your hair.

KAHLIL GIBRAN

DATE		

WHY I NEED TO UNPLUG TODAY:

_____

_____

_____

_____

_____

_____

_____

_____

_____

_____

_____

_____

_____

_____

_____

_____

_____

_____

_____

_____

DIGITAL DISTRACTIONS TO AVOID TODAY:

It was one thing to use computers as a tool, quite another to let them do your thinking for you.

TOM CLANCY

DATE		

WHY I NEED TO UNPLUG TODAY:

_____

_____

_____

_____

_____

_____

_____

_____

_____

_____

_____

_____

_____

_____

_____

_____

_____

_____

_____

_____

_____

_____

DIGITAL DISTRACTIONS TO AVOID TODAY:

We are like Hansel and Gretel, leaving bread crumbs of our personal information everywhere we travel through the digital woods.

———————

GARY KOVACS

DATE		

WHY I NEED TO UNPLUG TODAY:

_____

_____

_____

_____

_____

_____

_____

_____

_____

_____

_____

_____

_____

_____

_____

_____

_____

_____

_____

_____

_____

_____

_____

_____

DIGITAL DISTRACTIONS TO AVOID TODAY:

To be refreshed by a morning walk or an evening saunter ... to be thrilled by the stars at night; to be elated over a bird's nest or a wildflower in spring—these are some of the rewards of the simple life.

JOHN BURROUGHS

DATE		

WHY I NEED TO UNPLUG TODAY:

_____

_____

_____

_____

_____

_____

_____

_____

_____

_____

_____

_____

_____

_____

_____

_____

_____

_____

_____

_____

_____

_____

_____

_____

_____

DIGITAL DISTRACTIONS TO AVOID TODAY:

In general, I find that things that have happened to me out of doors have made a deeper impression than things that have happened indoors.

BERTRAND RUSSELL

DATE		

WHY I NEED TO UNPLUG TODAY:

_____

_____

_____

_____

_____

_____

_____

_____

_____

_____

_____

_____

_____

_____

_____

_____

_____

_____

_____

_____

_____

_____

_____

DIGITAL DISTRACTIONS TO AVOID TODAY:

I'm happier being outside the flow.

NICHOLSON BAKER

DATE		

WHY I NEED TO UNPLUG TODAY:

_____

_____

_____

_____

_____

_____

_____

_____

_____

_____

_____

_____

_____

_____

_____

_____

_____

_____

_____

_____

_____

_____

DIGITAL DISTRACTIONS TO AVOID TODAY:

That my complicated life could be made so simple was astounding.

CHERYL STRAYED

WHY I NEED TO UNPLUG TODAY:

_____
_____
_____
_____
_____
_____
_____
_____
_____
_____
_____
_____
_____
_____
_____
_____
_____
_____
_____
_____
_____
_____
_____
_____
_____

DIGITAL DISTRACTIONS TO AVOID TODAY:

At some point ... you gotta let go and sit still and allow contentment to come to *you*.

ELIZABETH GILBERT

WHY I NEED TO UNPLUG TODAY:

_____

_____

_____

_____

_____

_____

_____

_____

_____

_____

_____

_____

_____

_____

_____

_____

_____

_____

_____

_____

DIGITAL DISTRACTIONS TO AVOID TODAY:

In the spring, at the end of the day,
you should smell like dirt.

MARGARET ATWOOD

DATE		

WHY I NEED TO UNPLUG TODAY:

_____

_____

_____

_____

_____

_____

_____

_____

_____

_____

_____

_____

_____

_____

_____

_____

_____

_____

_____

_____

_____

_____

DIGITAL DISTRACTIONS TO AVOID TODAY:

People are locked up in all sorts of ways.

EMMA DONOGHUE

DATE		

WHY I NEED TO UNPLUG TODAY:

_____

_____

_____

_____

_____

_____

_____

_____

_____

_____

_____

_____

_____

_____

_____

_____

_____

_____

_____

_____

_____

_____

_____

DIGITAL DISTRACTIONS TO AVOID TODAY:

How beautiful it is to get up and go out and do something. We are here on Earth to fart around. Don't let anybody tell you any different.

KURT VONNEGUT

DATE		

WHY I NEED TO UNPLUG TODAY:

_____
_____
_____
_____
_____
_____
_____
_____
_____
_____
_____
_____
_____
_____
_____
_____
_____
_____
_____
_____
_____
_____
_____

DIGITAL DISTRACTIONS TO AVOID TODAY:

Then you're trapped in your lovely nest, and the things you used to own, now they own you.

CHUCK PALAHNIUK

	DATE	

WHY I NEED TO UNPLUG TODAY:

_____

_____

_____

_____

_____

_____

_____

_____

_____

_____

_____

_____

_____

_____

_____

_____

_____

_____

_____

_____

_____

_____

_____

_____

DIGITAL DISTRACTIONS TO AVOID TODAY:

The secret of contentment... lay in ignoring many things completely.

MARK HADDON

WHY I NEED TO UNPLUG TODAY:

_____

_____

_____

_____

_____

_____

_____

_____

_____

_____

_____

_____

_____

_____

_____

_____

_____

_____

_____

_____

_____

_____

_____

_____

_____

DIGITAL DISTRACTIONS TO AVOID TODAY:

If I knew I was going to die at a specific moment in the future, it would be nice to be able to control what song I was listening to; this is why I always bring my iPod on airplanes.

CHUCK KLOSTERMAN

DATE		

WHY I NEED TO UNPLUG TODAY:

_____

_____

_____

_____

_____

_____

_____

_____

_____

_____

_____

_____

_____

_____

_____

_____

_____

_____

_____

_____

_____

_____

_____

_____

DIGITAL DISTRACTIONS TO AVOID TODAY:

It was something every child knew how to do, maintain a direct and full connection with the world. Somehow you forgot about it as you grew up, and had to learn it again.

JEFFREY EUGENIDES

	DATE	

WHY I NEED TO UNPLUG TODAY:

_____
_____
_____
_____
_____
_____
_____
_____
_____
_____
_____
_____
_____
_____
_____
_____
_____
_____
_____
_____
_____
_____
_____

DIGITAL DISTRACTIONS TO AVOID TODAY:

Distracted from distraction by distraction.

T. S. ELIOT

DATE

WHY I NEED TO UNPLUG TODAY:

_____

_____

_____

_____

_____

_____

_____

_____

_____

_____

_____

_____

_____

_____

_____

_____

_____

_____

_____

_____

_____

DIGITAL DISTRACTIONS TO AVOID TODAY:

I like hanging around people who knit. They are usually in a good mood. People who are staring into their iPhones *and* demanding your attention at the same time are not as much fun.

MARK FRAUENFELDER

DATE		

WHY I NEED TO UNPLUG TODAY:

_____

_____

_____

_____

_____

_____

_____

_____

_____

_____

_____

_____

_____

_____

_____

_____

_____

_____

_____

_____

_____

_____

_____

_____

_____

_____

DIGITAL DISTRACTIONS TO AVOID TODAY:

O misery, misery, mumble and moan!
Someone invented the telephone,
And interrupted a nation's slumbers,
Ringing wrong but similar numbers.

OGDEN NASH

DATE		

WHY I NEED TO UNPLUG TODAY:

_____

_____

_____

_____

_____

_____

_____

_____

_____

_____

_____

_____

_____

_____

_____

_____

_____

_____

_____

_____

_____

_____

DIGITAL DISTRACTIONS TO AVOID TODAY:

The test of the machine is the satisfaction
it gives you . . . If the machine produces
tranquility it's right. If it disturbs you
it's wrong.

_____

ROBERT M. PIRSIG

DATE		

WHY I NEED TO UNPLUG TODAY:

_____

_____

_____

_____

_____

_____

_____

_____

_____

_____

_____

_____

_____

_____

_____

_____

_____

_____

_____

_____

_____

_____

_____

_____

_____

DIGITAL DISTRACTIONS TO AVOID TODAY:

On the big screen they showed us a sun / But not as bright in life as the real one / It's never quite the same as the real one.

BERNIE TAUPIN

WHY I NEED TO UNPLUG TODAY:

_____

_____

_____

_____

_____

_____

_____

_____

_____

_____

_____

_____

_____

_____

_____

_____

_____

_____

_____

_____

_____

_____

DIGITAL DISTRACTIONS TO AVOID TODAY:

We are deep in the era of the technological sublime, when awe can most powerfully be generated not by forests and icebergs but by supercomputers, rockets, iPods and particle accelerators. We are now continually awed by ourselves.

——————

ALAIN DE BOTTON

DATE		

WHY I NEED TO UNPLUG TODAY:

_____

_____

_____

_____

_____

_____

_____

_____

_____

_____

_____

_____

_____

_____

_____

_____

_____

_____

_____

_____

_____

_____

_____

DIGITAL DISTRACTIONS TO AVOID TODAY:

On the Internet, nobody knows you're a dog.

PETER STEINER

DATE		

WHY I NEED TO UNPLUG TODAY:

_____

_____

_____

_____

_____

_____

_____

_____

_____

_____

_____

_____

_____

_____

_____

_____

_____

_____

_____

_____

DIGITAL DISTRACTIONS TO AVOID TODAY:

And remember, the world is possibility if only you'll discover it.

RALPH ELLISON

	DATE		

WHY I NEED TO UNPLUG TODAY:

_____

_____

_____

_____

_____

_____

_____

_____

_____

_____

_____

_____

_____

_____

_____

_____

_____

_____

_____

_____

_____

DIGITAL DISTRACTIONS TO AVOID TODAY:

Step away from the device.

―――――

KNOCK KNOCK